My name is

Willow Althea Davis

I was baptized on

Sunday Aug. 4, 2013

My godparents are

Evy Nickerson

Thom Mason

This book is a gift from

Aunty Evy

My Baptism Book
2013 Eighth Printing this Edition
2012 Seventh Printing this Edition
2011 Sixth Printing this Edition
2010 Fourth and Fifth Printing this Edition
2009 Third Printing this Edition
2008 Second Printing this Edition
2007 First Printing this Edition

Text by Sophie Piper
Illustrations copyright © 2006 Dubravka Kolanovic
© 2006 Lion Hudson

The moral rights of the author and illustrator
have been asserted.

Published in the United States and Canada
by Paraclete Press, 2007.
ISBN: 978-1-55725-535-8
Originally published in English in 2006 by
Lion Hudson plc
Wilkinson House, Jordan Hill Road,
Oxford OX2 8DR, England

9 11 13 15 14 12 10 8

Acknowledgments
The unattributed prayers on pages 5, 6, 11, 13, 47, 48 and 50
are by Sophie Piper, copyright © Lion Hudson.
The unattributed prayers on pages 21, 24, 30 and 58 and those on
pages 36, 40, 49 and 53 are by Lois Rock, copyright © Lion Hudson.

Bible extracts are taken or adapted from the Good News Bible,
published by The Bible Societies/HarperCollins Publishers Ltd, UK
© American Bible Society 1966, 1971, 1976, 1992.

The Lord's Prayer (on page 44) from Common Worship: Services and
Prayers for the Church of England (Church House Publishing, 2000)
is copyright © The English Language Liturgical Consultation, 1988.

Prayer by Mother Teresa used by permission.

Published by Paraclete Press
Brewster, Massachusetts
www.paracletepress.com

Typeset in 16/24 Throhand Regular Roman
Printed and bound in China by Printplus Ltd. Year 2011.

My Baptism Book

Sophie Piper
Dubravka Kolanovic

PARACLETE PRESS
Brewster, Massachusetts

Me

I know I am me
from my head to my toes,
my hands and my fingers,
my ears and my nose.

Whatever I do
and whatever I'll be,
for ever and always
I know I'll be me.

Before I was made,
God loved me.

When I was born,
God loved me.

Now I am here,
God loves me.

For ever and ever
God loves me.

God, who made the earth,
The air, the sky, the sea,
Who gave the light its birth,
Careth for me.

God, who made the grass,
The flower, the fruit, the tree,
The day and night to pass,
Careth for me.

God, who made all things,
On earth, in air, in sea,
Who changing seasons brings,
Careth for me.

Sarah Betts Rhodes

Dear God
I know I am only little.
I can't be in charge of big things.
But I know I am safe with God:
as safe as a baby in its mother's arms.

From Psalm 131

Hand in hand
with someone who loves me
I feel safe.

Looking back
to someone who loves me
I feel safe.

Looking up
to the God who loves me
I feel safe.

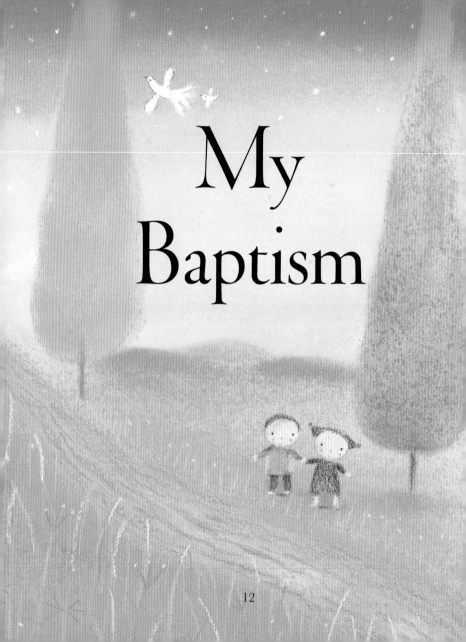

My
Baptism

I am baptized
to show that I am truly a child of God.

I am baptized
to show that I truly want to follow Jesus.

I am baptized
to show that I want God's Holy Spirit to
  be my friend and helper.

One day, some people brought their children to Jesus. They wanted him to give them his blessing.

Jesus' friends were angry. 'You mustn't waste Jesus' time,' they said. 'He's so busy preaching. The things he has to say are far too clever and far too important for children.'

Jesus called the children. 'Let the children come to me and do not stop them,' he said. 'The kingdom of God belongs to them.'

From Luke 18

Jesus told a story about a shepherd and his sheep.

Long ago, there was a shepherd who had one hundred sheep.

One day, a little lamb went missing.

The shepherd left the ninety-nine safe in the green pasture. He went to look for his lost lamb. He walked over the hills and along the valleys. The hours went by. The sun began to set.

At last the shepherd found his lamb. It had strayed a very long way. He was overjoyed to see it again. Gently he picked it up and carried it home.

When the lamb was safe with the flock, he called to his friends.

'I'm so happy!' he said. 'I have found my lost lamb. Please come to a party to celebrate.'

'God is like that shepherd,' said Jesus. 'When someone turns to God and asks to be brought back into the circle of God's love, all the angels sing for joy.'

From Luke 15

Angel of God, my guardian dear
To whom God's love commits me here,
Ever this day be at my side
To light and guard, to rule and guide. Amen.

Traditional

A Child of God

I wash my hands
to make them clean
and ready to do good.

And God above
will teach me how
to do the things I should.

Dear God
I say my prayers in the morning
when the golden sun begins to shine.

I ask you to show me what to do.
I ask you to help me be good.

I ask you to take care of me
and to keep me safe.

I ask you to bless me
and to make me happy.

From Psalm 5

We can do no great things,
Only small things with great love.

Mother Teresa of Calcutta

May my hands be helping hands
For all that must be done,
That fetch and carry, lift and hold
And make the hard jobs fun.

May my hands be clever hands
In all I make and do
With bricks and blocks, with sand and clay,
With paper, paint and glue.

May my hands be gentle hands
And may I never dare
To poke and prod and hurt and harm
But touch with love and care.

Whoever loves is a child of God...
for God is love.

1 John 4

I will love God with all my heart.
I will love God with all my soul.
I will love God with all my strength.

From Deuteronomy 6:5

I will love other people as much as
I love myself.

From Leviticus 19:18

I will love even the people who are unkind
to me. I will pray for them.

From Matthew 6

I will love the people who follow Jesus,
just as Jesus first loved us.

From John 13

God

O God,

as truly as you are our father,

so just as truly you are our mother.

We thank you, God our father,

for your strength and goodness.

We thank you, God our mother,

for the closeness of your caring.

O God, we thank you for the great love

you have for each one of us.

Julian of Norwich

White are the wavetops,
White is the snow:
Great is the One
Who made all things below.

Green are the grasslands,
Green is the tree:
Great is the One
Who has made you and me.

Blue are the cornflowers,
Blue is the sky:
Great is the One
Who made all things on high.

Gold is the harvest,
Gold is the sun:
God is our Maker –
Great is the One.

Dear God,

Thank you for being so good to us.

Thank you for listening to our prayers.

Thank you for the world we live in:

the summer and the winter,

the sunshine and the rain;

the time for sowing seeds

and the time to gather crops.

Thank you for all the good things the world

gives to us.

From Psalm 65

May all the world sing to our God!
The angels in the height,
the sun, the moon and silver stars
that glitter in the night;

The oceans and the giant whales,
the storms and wind and rain,
the animals and birds on every
mountain, hill and plain;

And all the people, young and old,
the wealthy and the poor:
sing praise to God who made the world,
sing praise for evermore!

From Psalm 148

Dear God, you are my shepherd,
You give me all I need,
You take me where the grass grows green
And I can safely feed.

You take me where the water
Is quiet and cool and clear;
And there I rest and know I'm safe
For you are always near.

Lois Rock, based on Psalm 23

Jesus

Jesus, friend of little children,
Be a friend to me;
Take my hand, and ever keep me
Close to thee.

Walter John Mathams

Let me travel to Christmas
By the light of a star.
Let me go to the hillside
Right where the shepherds are.
Let me see shining angels
Singing from heaven above.
Let me see Mary cradling
God's holy child with love.

Lois Rock

'Listen,' said Jesus. 'The only thing that really matters is being part of God's kingdom. Don't worry about anything else.

'Look at the wild birds. They don't worry about sowing seeds or gathering a harvest. They know that God will take care of them.

'Look at the wild flowers. They don't worry about making clothes. Yet God gives them petals that are more beautiful by far.

'If God cares so much about the birds and the flowers, you can be sure that God will take even more care of you.'

From Matthew 6

'When you pray,' said Jesus, 'say these words:

'Our Father in heaven,
hallowed be your name,
your kingdom come,
your will be done,
on earth as in heaven.
Give us today our daily bread.
Forgive us our sins
as we forgive those who sin against us.
Lead us not into temptation
but deliver us from evil.

'For the kingdom, the power
and the glory are yours
now and for ever.
Amen.'

'Listen,' said Jesus. 'The kingdom of God is like this.

'A person takes a tiny mustard seed and sows it in the ground.

'It grows into a tall tree. All the birds of the air come and make their nests in it.'

From Matthew 13

Dear God
Shelter me in the kingdom of your love.

Jesus was crucified.
He died and was buried.
God gave him new life.

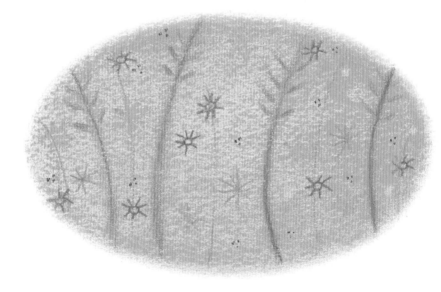

In the Easter garden
the leaves are turning green;
in the Easter garden
the risen Lord is seen.

In the Easter garden
we know that God above
brings us all to heaven
through Jesus and his love.

Lois Rock

Christmas is the time when angels open the gates
from heaven to earth:
I want to welcome heaven into my life.

Easter is the time when angels open the gates
from earth to heaven:
I want to follow Jesus into God's kingdom.

God's
Holy
Spirit

Let the Spirit come
like the winds that blow:
take away my doubts;
help my faith to grow.

Let the Spirit come
like a flame of gold:
warm my soul within;
make me strong and bold.

Lois Rock

Spirit of God
put love in my life.

Spirit of God
put joy in my life.

Spirit of God
make me good.

Spirit of God
make me kind.

From Galatians 5

May my life shine
like a star in the night,
filling my world
with goodness and light.

From Philippians 2

Blessings

May God bless you and take care of you.
May God be kind to you and do good
   things for you.
May God look on you with love and
   give you peace.

From Numbers 6

God the Father,
high in heaven,
hear my prayers
and come close to me.

God the Son,
high in heaven,
hear my prayers
and come close to me.

God the Holy Spirit,
high in heaven,
hear my prayers
and come close to me.

God bless all those that I love;
God bless all those that love me;
God bless all those that love those that I love
and all those that love those that love me.

From an old New England sampler

Lord, keep us safe this night,
Secure from all our fears;
May angels guard us while we sleep,
Till morning light appears.

John Leland

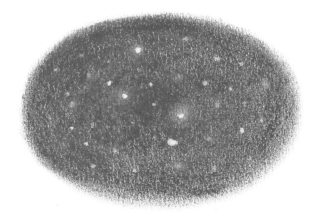

When I lie down, I go to sleep in peace;
you alone, O Lord, keep me perfectly safe.

From Psalm 4

Now I lay me down to sleep,
I pray thee, Lord, thy child to keep;
Thy love to guard me through the night
And wake me in the morning light.

Traditional

May the grace of the Lord Jesus be
with everyone.

Revelation 22 – the last line of the Bible